The Two Princesses

DIAN LAYTON
Artwork by Al Berg

DESTINY IMAGE® PUBLISHERS, INC.
P.O. Box 310, Shippensburg, PA 17257-0310
"Promoting Inspired Lives."

Illustrations by Al Berg

This book and all other Destiny Image and Destiny Image Fiction books are available at Christian bookstores and distributors worldwide.

For more information on foreign distributors, call 717-532-3040.
Or reach us on the Internet: www.destinyimage.com

ISBN 13 Hardcover: 978-0-7684-4389-9
ISBN 13 eBook: 978-0-7684-4388-2

For Worldwide Distribution, Printed in the U.S.A.
1 2 3 4 5 6 7 8 9 10 11 / 22 21 20 19 18 17

The Two Princesses

In the Kingdom of Human Heart there lived two princesses...
and they were sisters.
Their names were Quiet and Gentle Spirit
and Selfish Desire.

1

Selfish Desire was a beautiful girl with shining hair and long flowing gowns; but unfortunately she had a self-centered and very stubborn heart.

She filled every day doing things to make herself happy...spending hours in front of the mirror and commanding the castle servants to wait on her.

Quiet and Gentle Spirit was very different than her
sister. Although she was also beautiful, her real beauty
was in her kind, peaceful ways.

She filled every day doing things that would help other
people...spending hours making meals, singing songs
and playing games with the village children.

Everyone in the Kingdom of Human Heart
loved Quiet and Gentle Spirit.

In the Palace Beyond the Sea there lived a great and mighty King. One day the King sent his Messenger to the Kingdom of Human Heart, riding a white horse.

The Messenger blew a golden trumpet and read from a Royal Scroll:

Hear ye, hear ye, hear ye!
All princesses and young maidens are to prepare themselves —
for the King's only son, the Prince, is coming to choose a bride;
And behold, he is coming quickly!

As the Messenger galloped away, the Kingdom of Human Heart stirred with excitement. The Prince was coming to choose a bride! Quiet and Gentle Spirit and Selfish Desire, along with all the young maidens and princesses, hurried toward the Village to get their hair done and buy new dresses; the Prince was coming!

On their way to the Village, the maidens and princesses heard a loud groaning noise. There in the ditch lay a ragged man, loudly complaining of hunger and thirst. He didn't look very good...and he didn't smell very good. either. Selfish Desire sneered, held her nose and then led all the other maidens and princesses toward the Village.

But Quiet and Gentle Spirit hurried to the ditch.

"You poor man!" she exclaimed, helping him to his feet. "Come with me to the castle of the Kingdom of Human Heart. I will have the cooks fix you a good meal and something warm to drink. And we'll see about some new clothes...and...a bath, too. C'mon!"

After the man was taken care of and happily sitting by the fire, Quiet and Gentle Spirit set out once again for the Village. "I wonder what the prince looks like?" she thought, "I want to be ready to meet him. Hmmm...shall get a pink dress or a blue dress?"

Quiet and Gentle Spirit was just approaching the
Village when she noticed a man by the road; he was
crying. She gave him her handkerchief and gently
asked, "What's wrong? Why are you so sad?"

"Well...I'm new around here," he said, between sobs,
"I don't know anyone and I don't have any money and I
don't know where I'll stay tonight!"
Then the man paused for a moment before deciding to
continue, "But the main reason I'm sad...is...is
that I miss my teddy-bear!"
And with that, he cried even harder.

The princess patted his back reassuringly.
"Listen," she said, "There's plenty of room in the Castle of Human
Heart. You can stay in the royal guest room tonight and
I'll ask a servant to take you home in the morning.
And...I have an extra teddy-bear
that you can have to keep! Let's go!"

By the time the stranger had eaten supper and was
asleep in the royal guest room with his new teddy-bear
(which happened to be the princess's favorite teddy-bear),
it was too late to buy a dress;
the Village shops were closed.

"It's okay," said Quiet and Gentle Spirit with a yawn,
"The Messenger said the Prince is coming quickly...but
he won't come that quickly. I will get up very early in
the morning and get my hair done and buy a dress...

Hmmm...I wonder what the Prince looks like...?"
And with that, the princess fell asleep,
dreaming about the Palace Beyond the Sea.

The next morning, as the sun shone through her window and a rooster crowed, Quiet and Gentle Spirit jumped out of bed.

"Oh, no!" she exclaimed. "I just remembered; I can't go shopping today! Today is the day that I visit the prison and the hospital! I go the same day, every single week.
I take cookies and flowers and sing songs and...
and if I don't go, they will all be waiting for me;
I must go!
Let's see...there are cookies in the pantry,
I'll pick flowers on the way to the hospital,
I'll just stay for a few minutes...and then
I'll go get my hair done and buy a dress!"

And off she ran.

That day in the prison there was a new prisoner who was very grouchy and miserable. But when the princess gave him cookies, sang songs and talked to him about having a dream in his heart, the prisoner began to change! "You're right!" he said, "I do need a dream in my heart. Thanks for the advice...and thanks for the cookies."

"You're welcome," the princess called, hurrying to pick flowers for her friends at the hospital.

Quiet and Gentle Spirit quickly visited her friends at the hospital, and then, just as she was leaving, she noticed a new patient. He said that he had pain in his head, his throat was sore, his stomach was upset, and even his little toe was hurting. The princess fluffed up his pillow and patted his hand. After quite some time of reading words from the Great Book, the princess looked at the patient and suddenly remembered the Prince. Oh, no! She had spent far too much time here!

"I must go!" she said, quickly patting his hand again,
"I hope you get so much better that you're not even here
when I come next week. Good-bye! Good-bye!"

17

The princess ran down the road, her hair tangling in the wind and her dress getting torn and dusty. "Blue, pink, green – who cares what colour my new dress is, as long as it fits. And my hair; I must do something about my hair!"

The princess reached the first shop and was just about to go inside, when she heard the sound of the trumpet.

"Hear ye, hear ye, hear ye!" called the Messenger, "All young maidens and princesses are to appear immediately in the Castle Throne Room. The Prince has arrived!"

Quiet and Gentle Spirit turned from the shop door in surprise, "The Prince has arrived?! But I'm not ready. I'm not ready!"

Time seemed to stand still.

But then the princess wiped her eyes and smiled, remembering... "Oh, well. I'm really glad that I helped everyone. It's okay; the Prince wouldn't have chosen me anyway. Maybe he will choose Selfish Desire, because she's so pretty. But I wish...I wish I could have at least seen what he looks like...

Hey, why not?! I'll sneak into the Castle Throne Room and no one will notice me. I'll be able to see the Prince. I will see what he looks like!"

And off she ran to the castle.

The Throne Room was ringing with music and excitement
as Quiet and Gentle Spirit tiptoed into the background.
Beautiful maidens and princesses with lovely gowns and
shining curls were ready to meet the Prince.

Selfish Desire was looking into her mirror, as usual, when
she noticed her sister sneaking into the room. "Oh!" she
exclaimed, "How dare she appear like that? I'm shocked!
I'm also...gorgeous!" and she kissed her mirror lovingly.

Quiet and Gentle Spirit sighed and hid further in the shadows.
And then, at the command of the Messenger, all of the maidens and
princesses lined up on either side of a long carpeted aisle.

There, on the platform, stood the Prince. Quiet and Gentle Spirit
looked at the Prince...and she looked at him again...
there was something about his face, something about his eyes...
But wait! He had seen her! He was smiling! Oh, no!
A hush fell upon the room.

The prince stepped down from the platform and walked
down the long carpeted aisle. As he walked, the maidens
and princesses giggled and curtsied and giggled and
curtsied...but the Prince didn't look at any of them.
He walked right past Selfish Desire without even glancing her way.

He walked steadily toward the back of the room, toward a
princess with a tattered dress...and her eyes locked to his.

The Prince reached Quiet and Gentle Spirit and stood
before her. The princess fell to her knees, shocked and
embarrassed. The crowd held their breath.
Was the Prince angry that a princess had dared to come
into his presence looking like this?

But then...to the amazement of everyone, the Prince
helped Quiet and Gentle Spirit to her feet and lead her
out from the shadows...right to the centre of the room.
To the shock of the crowd and the wonder of the princess,
the Prince knelt down in front of her, and he began to sing:

"Quiet and Gentle Spirit – you have won my heart;
Quiet and Gentle Spirit – you have won my love.
I was hungry and you fed me;
I was thirsty you gave me a drink;
I was a stranger and you cared for me;
I was sick and in prison and you came to me.
Oh, Quiet and Gentle Spirit – your kindness has been seen;
Every time you helped someone...you were really helping me!"

Quiet and Gentle Spirit gasped. The man in the ditch...the stranger by
the road...the prisoner...the man in the hospital...each one had been
the Prince! He had disguised himself - because he wanted to know
who was the most beautiful girl in the Kingdom –
in her heart – where it counts.

The Prince stood to his feet.
He turned directly to Selfish Desire and the words
he spoke to her echoed throughout
the Kingdom of Human Heart:

"Selfish Desire, you must change – your heart, your
ways, your very name – to be Self-Less and not
Selfish; then true happiness will come your way."

The Prince reached out his hand and touched
Quiet and Gentle Spirit. In one miraculous moment,
in the twinkling of an eye, she was changed.
All of the beauty inside of her –
suddenly the world could see it.

She was clothed in a beautiful wedding gown,
her hair was lovely and shining...
and the Prince gently placed a new crown on her head.

And then the Prince took Quiet and Gentle Spirit home
to his Father's Kingdom. They were married...and they
ruled and reigned together forever, and ever and ever.

**And the best part about that story...
is that someday...it will come true.**